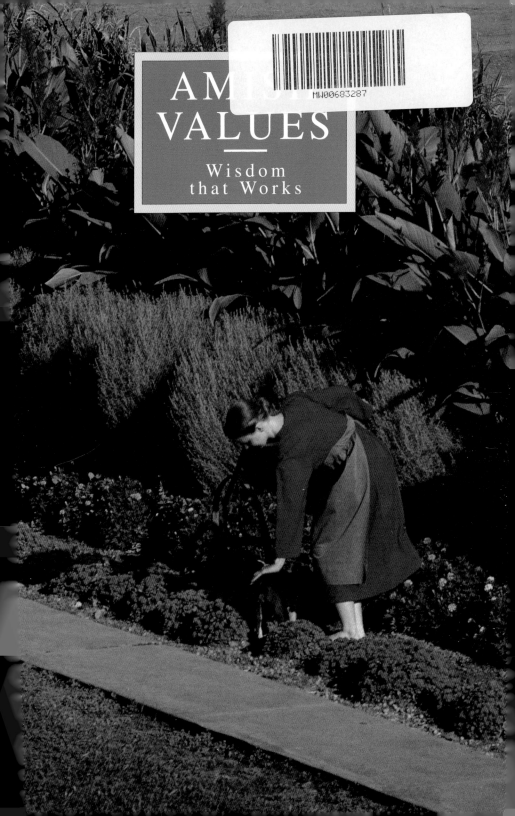

AMISH
VALUES

Wisdom that Works

Amish Values: Wisdom that Works
Text © 1995 by Ruth Hoover Seitz
Photography © 1995 by Blair Seitz
ISBN 1-879441-00-4

Library of Congress Catalog Card
Number 95-092701

Published by

RB
BOOKS

Seitz and Seitz, Inc.
1006 N. Second Street
Harrisburg, PA 17102-3121
Designed by Klinginsmith & Company

AMISH VALUES

Wisdom that Works

I·N·S·I·G·H·T·S

BOOKS
Harrisburg PA

Ruth Hoover Seitz

Photography by Blair Seitz

Introduction

There is an aura that I often feel at an Amish homestead. A sense of calm and rightness permeates the household. Work and play blend without the whir and hum of electrical appliances.

In the kitchen the ticking clock and its intermittent chimes are a dependable background sound. If we are in the garden, the steady sun and occasional moos of the cows surround us as we weed or pick. Sitting on the porch hulling peas to freeze or in the sitting room quilting holds contentment. I sense a flow of the present that is void of grandeur and grappling.

The work we are doing is purposeful and focused; I am neither bored nor pressed. I feel none of the performance anxiety that often taints my own hours at the word processor. The Amish do not deal with external standards for success because for them, the important things were long set by the church and tradition. The Amish are free because accumulating goods and recognition is irrelevant.

But the Amish are not unaware or insensitive. In the stream of Amish activities and relationships, what happens matters. One June day I dropped by to see an eighty-year-old retired farmer who had suffered a stroke and had not been driving his horse during the winter. When I asked about his health, Aaron smiled, "Quite good. I can't complain." It was reassuring to see him in his familiar chair.

As our talk turned to the productive spring rains, he mentioned that this had been the first year that he couldn't stoop to pick strawberries. I heard both acceptance and sadness in his voice. Aaron's yielding to his reality is as Amish as his self-sufficiency. He and his

left: On the farm the Amish practice faith close to God's earth.

above: On Sundays mules rest from farm work.

above: Pausing for conversation strengthens ties within the community.

wife cook their own meals in the *grossdaudi haus* (grandparent house) attached to the original farmhouse where their grandson's family now lives. The Amish have no retirement homes. Families rather than nursing homes care for the elderly.

My conversation with Aaron was interrupted by the arrival of a small lad in a straw hat, the typical summer head gear of Amish males. His head shyly dropped in my presence, but his great grandfather welcomed him to his knee. The boy offered him a small bag of bright red radishes, and then Aaron explained to me that the supply in the *daudi haus* was finished. Living in close proximity, extended families automatically share garden surplus and other small goodnesses of life.

There is often a surprise to relieve repetitive work. One summer afternoon Rachel and I were well into a row of peas, reaching deep into the bushes for the green, shiny pods. Because it was the first picking of the season, there so many white blossoms that we had to part the stalks with care. When the back-stretching task was approaching tedium, I heard the children

squeal with delight. The dog's barking in the adjoining wheat field had led them to a nest of newborn bunnies. The wiggly creatures stirred so much animated discussion that we quickly reached the end of the pea rows.

Large issues also arouse concern among Amish. Farming often stirs discussion because it is no longer the expected occupation of Lancaster's Amish from the beginning of this Pennsylvania settlement in the eighteenth century. About half of Lancaster County's Amish work on farms. With large families doubling the Amish population every twenty years and skyrocketing land prices squeezing financial viability out of farming, both the scarcity and the price of farms alarm the Amish. As a result, some Amish have migrated to other areas where land costs less.

But many more Amish have turned to other sources of income. For instance, as I wind through the rural countryside, I see signs offering homemade products or announcing a home-based business. A thousand of these enterprises, most small but successful, exist within this settlement of more than 18,000 Amish, according to Kraybill and Nolt in *Amish Enterprise: From Plows to Profits* (Baltimore: Johns Hopkins University Press, 1995).

With many more adult males working in small manufacturing firms or with construction teams, the Amish family faces more change than their grandparents could have imagined. One parent, not two, is at home during the day. For the entrepreneurs,

Below: Farming enables families to work together at home.

pleasing clients, employees and the government regulators is a new stress. There is increased exposure to non-Amish views. With such bombardments, members of this small religious community wrestle with remaining true to their Anabaptist beliefs that were carved out in the face of extreme persecution in the sixteenth century.

Today, they still strive to live out what they value. Ever since I began visiting the Amish in the 1980s, I have been struck with certain deep-seated beliefs and resulting practices. Like tendrils, their convictions take hold, influencing attitudes and choices in daily life.

I believe that these Amish ways hold value for others. But values are not a garb to be put on or a ritual to perform. They emerge from the inner will where a relationship with God spawns goodness expressed as love, honesty, kindness, humility, faith, and peace. My Amish friends would call these "Christian values," and many would chuckle at associating them with their particular sect. But I feel that the Amish blend of faith and culture gives us rare insights for living.

To safeguard the anonymity of the Amish I know, I have changed the names and slight details in the experiences shared here.

Above: All buggies in a settlement look the same.

right: Many Amish work at non-farm jobs.

right page: The Amish carriage represents simplicity.

1. Children are a gift from the lord.

Accept them as they come to you and train them with loving consistency.

Obedience tops the list of values that Amish parents want their children to learn. Sadie Beiler, mother of grown children, remembers "teaching the little ones to fold their hands in their laps at the table." This discipline, difficult for a hungry youngster, is a first step in expressing gratitude to God, the Amish ritual of pausing before a meal for silent grace. Parents view this step in toddlerhood as the touchstone for surrendering the individual's will to community goals.

A tow-headed almost-two-year-old repeatedly resisted "putting her hands down." Her parents, John and Anna Stoltzfus, did not overlook such stubbornness or delay this childhood lesson until their daughter Rebecca was more willing or mature. At dinnertime, John held his little one on his lap, enclosing her hands in his folded ones during grace. At supper, the evening

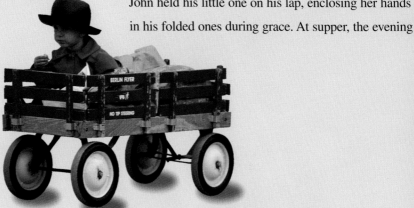

meal, he did the same. After several meals, Rebecca was again sitting at her own place on the bench folding her hands quietly under the table just like the rest of the family.

The Beilers found much more resistance in one child who continuously scrapped with her sibling. The parents talked quietly but fervently in Pennsylvania Dutch, the dialect that children learn first. They

above: Mother fills bottles with milk so that her sons can feed the calves.

left: Amish children help by loading shocks during the big task of threshing wheat.

remained patient but insistent, giving the attentiveness that the Amish assume parenting requires. From infancy that child heard no putdowns, only guidance and acceptance. "We look at raising children as a responsibility. Eventually, we see results," explained Jonas. "Some parts are more pleasant than others."

A child is not a family showpiece but a gift of God. Children are wanted but not adored. From birth, Amish children are accepted just as they are, complete with imperfections.

Guide young children, showing them how to comply. As children obey, they are enfolded into the family circle. They belong.

left: Care of animals teaches children responsibility and kindness.

right: Playing is fun in large Amish families, here on a trampoline at home.

2. "Running around" bridges the gap from childhood to adulthood.

Allow your teen children enough independence to test the values they gained in early years.

Even among the Amish, belonging to a community starts to feel restrictive to adolescents between the ages of 14 and 16, and their attitude shows that "they think they know a lot," comments a parent with much experience.

The Amish figuratively open the back door of their disciplined community so that youth from age 16 can "run around" or "try worldly ways" until they choose faith and baptism within the Amish Church.

With his own horse and buggy, a sixteen-year-old boy joins other teens–his "supper gang" for Sunday evening singing and games. At these group events, boys and girls do not arrive in couples but observe each other throughout the evening. Near the end, a young man may send a buddy to ask a young girl

whether she would go home in his friend's buggy. This may be the beginning of a special friendship. On the way home or in a letter that young man may ask to visit the girl at her home on a Saturday evening. Their time together in the "good room" may go quite late with an air of secrecy from family and friends.

For many Amish youth, evenings with their "supper gang" provide adequate breaking out, freedom from adult supervision.

But, as in other societies, some youth stretch the boundaries of what is permitted. They want to try lifestyle practices of the larger American society. They may install a radio in a buggy or even buy a car and go to movies, professional ball games or other popular amusements the Amish view as frivolous and worldly. Some parents would never permit the boom box that one youth bought for his room. And lounging at the local pool is not the usual way that Amish young women spend a summer afternoon. The Church overlooks the possibility that young adult males may experiment with concealing their Amish identity, even if only for one event.

Appearing non-Amish requires buying other clothes. And the desire for the money to experiment sets off another departure from the Amish way. Parents become uneasy when well-employed young people keep their paychecks rather than handing them over to the parents, who provide all necessities until marriage.

Amish parents draw limits for their children at varying points. Amos accepted that at 18, his son John would try some entertainment that would be foreign to his life as a 30-year-old married man. However,

below: Playing volleyball is an acceptable "supper gang" activity.

left: A carriage of Amish young people travels to a home to socialize.

next pages: These young men use a horse-drawn wagon to take their canoes to the river.

Stephen's father assumed that his son would follow the Amish practices throughout his youth with only pranks and late nights indicative of his breaking out towards adulthood.

As teens approach their twenties, parents pray and voice concern that their offspring "join church," which precedes marriage. When young people decide to "believe in Christ as their own personal Savior" and to tell the ministers that they want to become church members, they are giving up their worldly spirit. Jonas remembers his mother standing at the bottom of the

stairs pleading for him to do right, even as he got ready to go out with his friends. One minister explains, "We just hope that they'll turn around and come into the Church."

And most do. Four out of five children remain Old Order Amish. Those who don't frequently join other "plain churches" following Christian principles and keeping family ties. In the instances when a teen chooses a secular lifestyle outside the fold, the parents never stop praying. "We hope," explained one woman, "but it's like a wound that never closes."

Allow teens to practice and test the values that they were taught, but stay in touch lest their sailing become drifting. It is tempting to launch youth into adulthood too soon.

left: Young women belonging to the same "buddy bunch" or age group wade in a creek.

right page: As young people work together, here planting seedlings, they firm the bonds that draw them to become members.

3. Parents and their grown children are a blessing to each other.

Grandparents and parents, be wise in assisting as well as in withholding assistance. Engender love and trust.

In the Amish community extended families often live on the same piece of land with each household planting its own garden. Eighty-one-year old Jonas bought a farm 58 years ago; four generations now live on it. His grandson's family works the land and lives in the main farmhouse while Jonas and his sixty-year-old son head two other households on this 80-acre farm.

Over the decades, members of each generation play varying roles. For example, parents participate fully in the marriage preparations of their children. The church has set the order of the wedding, and the parents dip into their savings and provide for the new household. After a November wedding, the newlyweds return to the homes of their individual families to finalize everything for "setting up housekeeping" around April 1, the beginning of a new season. The couple receives enough provisions to tide them over until their own garden is producing.

For most parents, "a good start" also includes a dowry or *aussteier* of household goods that is at least as complete as the one *they* received when they were starting out. Many brides receive a corner cupboard and sideboard as well as a table and chairs. Beds, quilts and blankets come from both families with a horse and buggy brought to the marriage by the husband. If parents can, they give financial assistance so that their sons can get into farming or business.

When John and Anna Stoltzfus married, they moved into a new wing built onto his parents' homestead. A year later when John took over his father's farm, that addition became the *daudi haus* for the older Stoltzfuses.

below: Two generations plant tobacco.

next pages: Additions to an Amish house enable several generations to live on the same property.

Anna cherishes the kindness of her mother-in-law, who accepted her moving into a house and setting up a kitchen the older woman had managed for decades. Simultaneously, John's father refrained from giving unsolicited advice to his son, who took over the home farm. The graciousness of the aging parents

encouraged John and Anna to give their utmost to the challenge of "making a go of farming." It is wrenching for parents to see their offspring struggle to gain a farm. To illustrate the financial burden of farming in Lancaster County, one minister explained that his son invested as much in his cows and dairy as he had put into everything, including the land.

John's parents cook their own meals in their own quarters. As the parents age, their children gradually do more of the yard work, and the little ones run errands for their grandparents. Living at close range is a blessing of both love and convenience that holds them all in a family security blanket.

In one Amish family in the nineties, the middle generation was astute in building a *grossdaudi haus* on their property but not connected to the main house. "We're not quite ready for that even though my parents need a place," explained the mother of four teens.

Among the Amish, responsibility ebbs and flows between generations. The family is a home for individuals from birth to death.

above: Harvesting wheat demands the help of all.

right page: Traveling 5 mph by horse and buggy prompts the old and the young to live near each other.

Aging parents, trust your offspring, honoring the way your grown children handle responsibilities during the prime of life. Parents between two generations, sprinkle kindness on the young and the old so that harmony will increase.

4. Visiting strengthens ties between people.

Take time to visit and have fun with family and friends.

I n Amish communities, families visit each other without giving advance notice or receiving an invitation.

Visiting is a Sunday activity that honors the Sabbath as a day free of all but necessary work. One woman with eleven grown children recalled that when the children were young, after church they dropped in to visit her brothers and sisters or in-laws. "The children liked being with their cousins. Sometimes the older children stayed home to do the milking and feeding while we took the young ones along."

And her grown children still visit. Young families sometimes travel to the church services of their friends in another district. During and after the fellowship meal that regularly follows the church service, they socialize.

For the Amish, talking face to face is far superior to phone conversation. Safeguarding the practice of visiting is one of the reasons that the Old Order Amish forbid having a phone in the house. One mid-age woman who has a phone in her barn for her market business confessed that she and her sister, who lives a four-hour car-ride away, talk one hour each Friday morning. I laughed when her sister showed up without warning one Friday about the time they usually phone. Visiting takes precedence.

Two spring holidays, Ascension Day and Pentecost, provide all-day occasions to socialize with the extended family or friends. The day is for rest. Just like Sunday, there's no work in the fields and shops. But on these holidays the Amish in many communities go fishing or play baseball–activities that are taboo on Sunday.

On one Ascension Day, a commemoration of Christ's return to Heaven, a three-generation Amish family set out a picnic beside a community creek. After lunch, the females of all ages took a walk downstream and gathered some meadow tea. The men played quoits, tossing steel donuts onto a ring in a game similar to horseshoes. Young boys inline skated on the macadam road. A horse grazed under a shade tree until it was time to load the buggy and go home to milk the cows.

Such family events pile up an accumulation of good memories. The Riehl cousins play in the cornfield

above: A family goes visiting with a scooter packed in with the children.

left page: A family picnics on Ascension Day, a religious holiday from work.

next pages: Letters and visits keep the Amish in touch with each other.

rows. When the pond is frozen, many children skate. One father told me of a late Sunday night shuffleboard competition between the young men and their fathers. Within the Amish world, fun activities build skills as well as a sense of personal well-being.

"A person who does a lot of visiting" is well-liked. The Amish say that taking time to go see someone means that you care. The talk covers news of relatives and friends as well as social plans. What is happening in the township may also arouse interest. However, an Amish person does not converse about efforts at self-improvement or boast about new purchases. Visiting firms each Amish person's place in the community.

Make visiting important in your family life. When people say, "Let's get together" or "Come over," do. If they are surprised, tell them how much you enjoy getting together, and do it again.

left: An Amish family picnics.

right page: This buggy provides an open-air ride.

32.

5. Working with the soil holds value.

Let your hands feel the life in the land. Tend a plant, a garden or a farm to stay connected to the earth's growth cycle.

The Amish feel linked to the earth at many levels. Women design and plant colorful beds of flowers near their houses, barns and vegetable gardens. Farm families do their work according to the rhythm of the seasons, using superb organizational skills to meet the demands of their crops and stock. Experience builds a farmer's finesse in each area. For instance, making hay requires judging its maturity and dryness as well as storing it properly. And these skills are preceded by knowledge of preparing the soil, planting the seeds and controlling weeds. Said one Amish farmer, "Work in agriculture expands your mind; it is just like college."

Another Amish man rates experience with plants and animals as essential. "If people are foreign to God's world in nature," claims Jonathan, "they lose who they are." This carriage shop owner raises his family of eight children on four acres close to a busy borough. To learn responsibility, these youngsters care for 200 chickens and two cows. They make and peddle butter, eggs and produce along a regular route. The children get up at five o'clock, even on school days. The father feels that this routine "helps my children face the realities of responsibility–that it is always there."

above: Children hoe tobacco, a labor-intensive crop, while their father cultivates the soil between the rows.

Every Amish child understands hoeing and the importance of mulching to reduce weeding. They learn at a young age that crops must be harvested when they're ready, that everything has its season.

The bottom line stated by some Amish is, "If you cannot farm, grow what you eat. Eat out of the garden rather than the store."

Give children the privilege of caring for plants until they produce a flower or food to eat. Observe how tending the earth and the passing of time work together during the growing season.

above: A couple brings in corn for fodder.

right page: Amish women do fieldwork, here hauling alfalfa bales.

6. A family that works together grows together.

Share the household responsibilities to add to the quality of your life together.

An Amish family faces a daily work agenda that is foreign to an American household where most needs are supplied through stores or mail order houses. For the Amish, clothing and feeding a family include sewing their traditional garb and growing foods to preserve. Many keep the house and garden clean and trimmed to a standard close to perfection. In an Amish household, there is work to do all day every day.

A family working together lives out a work ethic that has been the backbone of Amish tradition. It implies that even the youngest can help. Sharing responsibilities such as picking vegetables or milking

above: A family puts in a garden in the early spring.

below: Beautiful flower gardens result from much care.

next pages: An Amish farm provides tasks for the whole family.

twice each day draws a family together. Each member knows what the other is about, and the layers of hours together create a firm closeness. The love and the respect woven between parents and young children, says one Amish woman, make them as teens less apt to "grieve their parents before they join the church."

(After baptism, church membership signals the strict compliance with Amish practices. If a member of the church goes astray and refuses to confess, the member is shunned. The fallen one cannot eat or do business with other members. Because of the isolating power of this ban, Amish seriously fulfill their religious obligations. One man told me that shunning is a factor in keeping adultery and the possibility of divorce very far from Amish families.)

Mary Sue Yoder said that as a mother she practices three parenting principles that taught her children to work. "First, it's good to work with them, for instance, in the garden or in the kitchen, instead of telling the children how to do it." A parent conveys a positive attitude toward the task and models a level of performance for the child to reach.

"Second, when a child likes to do a certain thing, let him go with that responsibility." Mary Sue remembers that one of her sons who now works with his hands making wood furniture would grab a beater and want to help with the baking. "Because of his interest, he got jobs in the kitchen."

"Third, a child's interest grows when he has to do a

39.

above: By participating from a young age, boys learn how to harvest grain.

right page: Grandfather oversees the early morning work on a dairy farm.

job often. How can he learn something well if he only gets experience occasionally?" With her eight children, Mary Sue assigned regular responsibilities so each child could "own" the task. For example, when her youngest started sweeping the kitchen after breakfast, he missed some crumbs, but gradually he became more thorough and noticed the improved results of his effort.

Amish families garden and preserve produce together. Husband and wife prepare and plant the plot together. During wheat harvest in early July and tobacco cutting in September, the whole family invests energy into a major field effort. Families also join together to clean the school yard and classroom. With each event, Amish people attach more deeply as a community, belonging in a way beyond measure.

Plan and work together on projects that will benefit the household and nurture the family's sense of togetherness.

7. Having fancy and abundant possessions crowds out a clear, simple lifestyle that can support relationships and develop inner moral strength.

Choose to live with simplicity rather than clutter and luxury.

The Amish live according to the rules of the *Ordnung*, an unwritten but specific prescription for behavior. These guidelines do not abolish convenience or disapprove of comfort but they embrace plainness, thrift and identity. For example, Jake asked his non-Amish neighbor for the bucket seat from a parts car, so he could be more comfortable while he was plowing. Using a modern car part is acceptable but driving a car is forbidden. The purpose of any prohibition is to safeguard their separateness from a society that the Amish consider worldly. It stems any push for individual success and pleasure by drawing boundaries to make it easier for the Amish to follow their community's Bible-based aims.

For instance, the Old Order Amish do not use inflated tires and thus do not ride bicycles which seem like a simple, planet-friendly mode of transportation. On a bicycle, however, a child could quickly get far from home, the heart of Amish life. Using scooters and horse-drawn carriages and wagons keeps brakes on the distance the Amish travel. It supports home-centered living.

For the Amish, it's easy to decide what to wear, how to travel and how to furnish the house. Dressing uniformly in clothes made of solid-colored fabric removes the competitive realm of fashion from their lives. The adult men grow beards with their hair cut straight, not layered, just below the ears. Life is

above: An Amish country-side reflects simplicity.

next pages: Amish schools reflect the same simplicity observable in their homes and attire.

right page: Amish children know what they will wear and do not worry about rejection because of their clothing.

below: Grave markers are simple in style and inscription.

simpler with no choice of hair style or length. The *Ordnung* forbids air travel and driving a car. The only pictures on the walls of Amish homes are small ones attached to calendars. In various areas of life, adornment is a culprit that may lead the Amish into luxuries and frivolities.

The Amish do make money, some building spacious brick homes with kitchens with extensive cabinetry. Those who are financially well-off eat out more frequently and take road trips in hired vans, usually visiting relatives in other Amish settlements. An article in *Family Life*, a magazine that promotes spiritual and "plain living" and reaches many Amish homes, urged people with means to assist struggling young farm families rather than buy new furniture or other luxuries.

In Amish society, silence gathers people. The absence of radio, TV, telephone and a CD player creates a quiet environment that is an opening for a family to converse, joke or play table games. In religious life, a regular silent prayer during the church service draws the community into humility and bareness before God.

Contemplate simplicity. Make purchases that enhance rather than overwhelm relationships in your household.

8. In a spirit of humility, the Amish try to achieve without being proud.

Focus on accomplishing a task in fine order, honoring yourself, your family and your community.

he Amish readily voice appreciation for completing or achieving. Anna spent several years making custom window treatments. She enjoyed managing this cottage industry which produced income for several family members and brought her satisfaction. It was a delight to see curtains and drapes that she installed fit well. Now retired, Anna is clear that pride was not part of her sense of achievement.

One Amish leader confirms that the line between this inner delight and pride is very thin. Sermons warn against being "big feeling" or proud. The Amish way is to voice opinions softly and to give without fanfare. For instance, they give alms, money for those in need, in the following way. Twice a year on communion Sunday, a deacon stands at the door of the home where church was held. As members file out, they place bills in the pockets of his vest, coat and pants. One leader recommends, "Having your bills folded in your pocket before you arrive will keep others from seeing how much you are giving. In Matthew 6 in the Bible we are told to give 'in secret.'" The deacon keeps changing the pocket where he places each contribution so that he cannot remember who gave what.

To give attention or publicity to an accomplishment makes pride public. Parents refrain from over-emphasizing a child's individual successes or good deeds. After the prayer before dinner, a little child broke the silence with the announcement that she had been quiet. She looked at her mother for recognition of her obedience. No one gave it to her. She had done as she had been taught, and praise was unnecessary. The potatoes were passed and the meal begun.

In the Amish parochial school, often one-room, there are no academic awards. A teacher commends

left page: Clothes promote equality rather than pride.

below: Alone with his land, a man harrows his field so his crop will grow well.

scholars for completing their work well but does not set up competitions that focus on striving for superiority of one above the other. A high point for students is a treat from the teacher for the whole room or school. One teacher invited all of the children's families to a chicken barbecue at her home–a gesture that supported the school as a part of the religious community.

The Amish make decisions in the context of their community commitment. They weigh how a choice will be viewed by others in their family and church district. Rachel uses her artistic skills to make products that bring in family income. When she wanted a rock garden in her backyard, she took time off from her business to do it herself. Hiring a landscaper would have been a better economic decision, but Rachel wanted to appear thrifty, not wealthy. She also enjoyed digging in the dirt herself! She did not view this consideration for the values of her community as restrictive people pleasing.

The Amish value humility and meekness, often to the point of speaking softly and slowly. This demeanor grows out of a deep belief that they are the servants of God living on earth to do God's will, not to promote themselves.

right page: Ingenuity is valued when it contributes to the family or community.

below: Amish women express creativity by planting flower beds.

Gain inner satisfaction from reaching goals that complete your self and your community. Avoid self-aggrandizement in order to honor God more fully.

52.

9. With nurture, virtue grows inside the heart and forms a moral blueprint for living. How people act says more about their faith than what they say they believe.

Tap into spiritual resources that keep your moral stance strong, even in the face of difficult situations.

I t is a misunderstanding to think that practices such as dressing plain and driving a horse and buggy create Amishness. The most important foundation of Amish life is believing the Bible and practicing what the Church teaches. Sunday sermons and daily prayers point to virtues and principles that belong in daily actions.

The Amish gain moral understanding from sermons delivered in German during the bi-weekly Sunday service. Before eight o'clock in the morning Amish families walk or drive their buggies to one of the homes in their church district. They listen to sermons in German that feature Bible stories and guidelines and teach the Amish way.

In one service, the minister taught the importance of practicing gratitude by telling the following story. "During hay harvest, a farmer took off his hat every time he brought a load into the back of his barn.

left: At Sunday church held in homes, the Amish hear sermons on how to practice their faith.

"Why do you take off your straw hat, papa?" his young son asked.

"I'm thanking God."

"For each load?" the little boy wondered.

"No, for each bale."

Although they view God as the Giver of all, the Amish do not talk about God granting them desires or special blessings that favor their financial or economic situation. They believe the Bible explanation that "the rain falls on the just and the unjust." For them, the events of the universe–positive and negative–are within God's domain.

When bad things happen, the Amish analyze the strength of their faith rather than God's reason for allowing it. "We don't try to outguess God; we tend to recite Scriptures such as, 'All things work together for good to them that love God..,'" explained one woman.

"But when my aunt, a woman who was like a mother to me, was brutally murdered by a neighbor, none of the usual comforting words took care of my grief. One bishop assured our family that God

55.

understood because His own son, Jesus, had been killed. He confirmed God's care. Eventually, I accepted that even in an act so foreign to our culture, God is present and just as strong. How would I have coped without faith in God?"

Their religious community offers solutions when financial difficulties stress Amish families. Crop failure or medical expenses may threaten a family's solvency. When costs exceed a family's capability, Amish Church Aid assists with hospital bills because the Amish do not take out medical insurance and frown on accepting government aid. A family that cannot surface above their debts can tell their minister, who will appoint trustees to work out a financial plan and oversee payments. This solution is humbling because the committee takes over the family checkbook. One man who is frequently asked to help because of his financial acumen–"he can make one dime do the job of two"–found that a family that follows these outside recommendations, however painful, can usually forego bankruptcy and "get on sound footing again."

The Amish believe gaining spiritual growth through God and a caring community can happen in good and bad times.

above: The Amish demonstrate their faith by helping to raise a barn.

right page: The Bible, here a German edition, provides guidelines for living.

Develop faith and exercise moral traits that build character that will enable you to be strong and caring.

Des blutigen Schauplatzes

oder

Märtyrer=Spiegels

der

Taufs=Gesinnten

oder

Wehrlosen Christen

Zweiter Theil.

Vormals in Holländischer Sprache herausgegeben und mit vielen glaubwürdigen
Urkunden versehen.

Nun aber sorgfältig übersetzt und mit einigen neuen Nachrichten vermehrt.

PUBLISHED BY SHEM ZOOK, NEAR LEWISTOWN, MIFFLIN COUNTY, PA.

Philadelphia:
PRINTED BY KING & BAIRD, No. 9 SANSOM STREET.
1849.

10. Learning is far more valuable than education.

Gain information that is useful to you and your community.

I have observed that the Amish highly regard learning, not for its own sake but for improving their income-generating skills and for deepening their spiritual understanding. Illiteracy is virtually non-existent in their settlements. Because they have no exposure to other media, the Amish spend much more time reading than most Americans. Many subscribe to *Readers Digest, Farm Journal* and religious publications.

The Amish are adept at gaining specific information to reach their goals. Many view themselves as lifelong learners.

A tourist was talking with 14-year-old Jacob, who had just completed eighth grade and would be attending vocational school (3 hours per week and journal-keeping on his farm work) for another year. This program, a substitute for public high school, is government-approved since a 1972 Supreme Court decision.

The visitor watched Jacob wash a cow's udders,

above: Amish schools support Amish ways.

above: The Amish value learning by doing.

above: The mail brings magazines that the Amish read, often with relish.

wondering if the Amish teen felt deprived by his community's practice. Then he asked, "Wouldn't you like to go to school longer?"

The response was quick and firm, "No."

"I went to school 21 years," explained the visitor, a college professor.

The youth stopped milking and tilted his head to look the man in the eye. "You must know everything."

"Oh, no, I'm learning all the time," responded the professor.

The lad pushed the cow's swishing tail aside and said matter-of-factly, "Well, that's what we do too, learn as we go along."

The Amish refer to one of them who likes to learn as "a reader." Motivated by keen interest, an Amish person may delve wholeheartedly into a subject. Individuals have explored such areas as alternative

60.

medicine, nutrition, organic horticulture and machine tooling.

The Amish commonly learn by doing. They agree with the saying, "More is caught than taught." Fathers thoughtfully field their sons out to work with skilled craftsmen or highly regarded farmers because they know that their boys will bring back well-honed skills. Daniel told me that apprenticeship served his sons well. "They didn't get paid, but they learned over time and could see if their interest in a field would hold." Placing children in shops operated by other Amish keeps youth in the community throughout the work week.

above: End-of-year school picnic underlines family support of learning.

next pages: When Amish children complete their formal schooling at age 14, they enter life with the skills to make a living.

The Amish are inclined to pursue inventions or systems that will solve a local problem. One young man devised equipment to make methane gas and organic compost from manure. Another invented a gauge to record the gas in a silo; this device saved many lives.

The Amish attach learning to life rather than courses. Their self-education is purposeful.

Cultivate learning to improve your life, your family and your neighborhood.

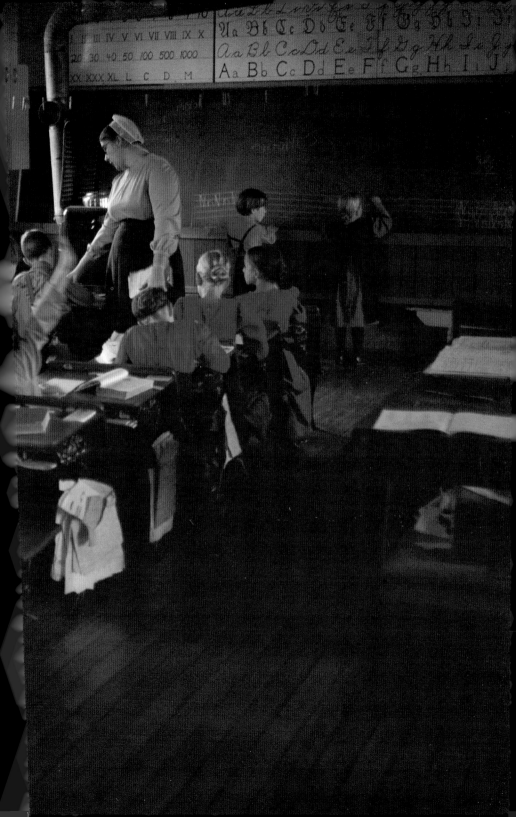

THE END

Living in 227 settlements in 23 U.S. states and
Canada, the Amish struggle to live their
values. For those of us in society's main-
stream, living the italicized guidelines in this
book are challenging. Gains may come slowly.
Assess your inner growth as one aging Amish
man did his pace: "I can do part of a day's
work, but it may take a week to do it."

Ruth Hoover Seitz